HOW TO LOVE YOUR BUSINESS

How to
LOVE
Your
BUSINESS

Stop Recreating Trauma and
Have a Business You Love —
and That Loves You Back

Nicole Lewis-Keeber

ISBN 978-1-7367981-0-2

Also available as an ebook: 978-1-7367981-1-9

This book is dedicated to the Inner Kiddo CEO's

CONTENTS

Introduction

If anyone had told me three years ago that I would be writing a book about business, much less one about people's relationships with their businesses, I would have questioned their sanity. What does it even mean to have a business that you love and that loves you back?

Yet here we are. It turns out I am passionate about this topic. So passionate that I have dedicated my own time and resources to this—because, guess what? It changes lives. It changed mine. It continues to change my clients' lives and the lives of anyone who hears me speak about it. That's why I have written this book—to help as many people as possible.

Every day I see business owners and entrepreneurs who are stressed out by their businesses. They feel overwhelmed by their schedules, alone and unsupported. The financial freedom that they were seeking by becoming their own bosses has eluded them. The pressure to get things right and take care of a myriad of tasks feels like a boulder pressing down on their chests. They feel run down and beaten up.

They internalize the problems in their businesses, becoming so miserable that they seek relief by reading self-help books and working on their mindset. But it doesn't help. They end up feeling worse because their efforts still do not get them the results that they'd hoped for.

What they haven't realized is that no one drops their personal baggage at the door when they start a business. In fact, starting a business means entering into a relationship, just like a friendship, a romance, or a neighborly or familial relationship. And just like in human-to-human relationships, if we do not set clear boundaries, and work to practice them mindfully, we are bound to default into toxic behaviors from our past. In other words, we bring our emotional challenges into our businesses with us, and when we ignore this, we get in trouble.

This book is based on my experience as a therapist and coach working with small business owners and entrepreneurs. It's designed to help you identify your disempowering patterns so you can change the dynamic you have with your business, clients, partners and yourself. I know you can do it, because I have done it myself—both in my business and in my personal life. There is "no shame in my game." I have been married three times. I created the same dynamic again and again, until I found clarity and changed my paradigm. I am now happily married and there is no damn way I am falling into that trap again. I could tell early on that this man was worth the personal work it would take to change my mindset and create a lasting relationship.

Just as we recreate patterns in our personal relationships, we often recreate them in our relationship with our business. In this book, I share the exact moment when I realized that I had created a business that was demanding and demeaning instead of loving and supportive. But I don't stop there. I also share how my background as a survivor of child abuse and my training as a therapist gave me the clarity to identify that I was recreating trauma within the very structures that I'd thought would bring me freedom, and what I did to heal and reverse that.

In this book, I share the processes that I used to transform myself and my work, and how they have also helped my clients do the same. I outline the steps for creating an Emotional Sustainability Plan that will yield a business that you love and that loves you back.

If you are feeling burdened and overwhelmed, I'll help you remember when in your life you have felt this way before. I'll help you identify who your business is standing in for. Is it that mean 8th grade teacher you had, a demanding father, or your first mean boss? Once you can see what role you are playing in your business—and what role your business is playing in your life—you will be able to change it so that you can make more money, feel more connected to your business and your clients, and have a business that is emotionally sustainable.

This book helps you to locate your own story and identify the characters in it. But most importantly, it helps you change who the characters are and what they do, and write new chapters for yourself, so you can have the business—and the life—you love.

You gotta go through it to get to it, so buckle up and jump in.

♥ ♥ ♥

Chapter One

Your Relationship to Your Business

Have you ever experienced a moment when you felt like giving up? When you were at such a low point that you couldn't see your way out? When you had a choice to either quit or make one next right step to try to save yourself? Me, too.

I want to tell you about the moment when I almost gave up on my business and my dreams.

I remember that morning clearly. I had been in business for about two years providing money-mindset coaching to small business owners and entrepreneurs. I had never been a business owner prior to my coaching business, so I had a pretty steep learning curve. I was a business of one and if something needed to be done, it was up to me to do it.

I had been juggling way too much at once—learning business management, sales, marketing, copywriting, coaching clients, networking, and social media. At the same time, I was testing and changing my approach on how money and trauma are connected. To say I was worn out would be an understatement. I was feeling frustrated and beat up. Worse, I felt like I was letting people down. I couldn't complete all of my daily tasks, I was not as available to my clients as I thought I should be, and I felt I was letting my husband down because my business wasn't growing as fast as I thought it would. This was not the business that I had signed up for.

One morning I woke up at 5 a.m. feeling like a failure. Nothing was working out and I was exhausted. I was at war with myself, and as I lay in the dark beside my sleeping husband, I considered closing my business. As far as I saw it, my options were to give in and quit, or try to change something so I could get through this unending struggle.

I got up, went into the kitchen, and put the coffee on. As I waited for it to brew, I pulled out Elizabeth Gilbert's book *Big Magic* and opened to a random chapter. I was hoping for some inspiration or—at the very least—a distraction from the itty bitty shitty committee "chorus of negative voices" that had convened in my head.

It was a story about botanist and author Dr. Robin Wall Kimmerer, a professor at SUNY College of Environmental Science and Forestry. The passage, towards the end of *Big Magic,* describes a moment in her environmental biology class each year where she asks her students two questions. The first is, "Do you love nature?" to which all hands go up. The second, "Do you believe that nature loves you in return?" elicits the opposite response. All hands go down. At which point Robin says, "Then we have a problem already." Gilbert writes, "These earnest young world-savers honestly believe that the living earth is indifferent to them." She goes on:

> Ancient people did not see it this way, needless to say. Our ancestors always operated with a sense of being in a reciprocal emotional relationship with their physical surroundings. Whether they felt that they were being rewarded by Mother Nature or punished by her, at least they were engaged in a constant *conversation* with her. Robin believes that modern people have lost that sense of conversation—lost that awareness of the earth communicating with *us* just as much as we are communicating with *it*. Instead, modern people have been schooled to believe that nature is deaf and blind to them—perhaps because we believe that nature has no inherent sentience. Which is a somewhat pathological construct, because it denies any possibility of relationship.

Without that sense of relationship, Kimmerer says, her students are missing out on something incredibly important: Their potential to become *co-creators* of life.

While reading that story, I had an epiphany. What Dr. Kimmerer emphasizes is that it is not only possible to have a relationship with a non-sentient being—it's a worthwhile project. Not only that, we can expect and demand that the entity—be it nature, your house, or your business—love you back. It was an *aha!* so epic that it changed the course of my business and my life. As I read the story I was saying to myself, "I love my business, but I don't feel like it loves me back. In fact, I feel like my business hates me and is terrorizing me."

I then asked myself this question: "If I am feeling abused by my business, did *I* set it up to do that?"

The answer was so clear to me that it took my breath away: I had recreated old patterns of abuse from my childhood within the structures of my business. In essence—and unconsciously—I had shaped my business to function as an abuser.

This was the divine moment where all of the puzzle pieces started to connect for me.

But, of course, I wasn't done. I had to ask myself how this had happened. As a therapist, I knew that childhood trauma creates patterns of behavior that continue to play out in future relationships. It is not uncommon for abused people to pick up the work of the abuser, by then engaging in self abusive patterns. We use food, substances, work, and relationships to recreate the messed-up patterns we experienced. It was clear to me that I had done this: I had let my business take over where my mom had left off.

In my mother's eyes, I could do nothing right. She gave no positive feedback. She kept moving the finish line so that what success meant was always changing. She was demanding and demeaning. I could never be right or experience satisfaction. In my business, I started each work day by giving away my power to an invisible "they" (some days "they" was several people, while other days it was one specific person). "They" directed me in a way that could derail one project or my entire business. "They" became my mom all over again. I had let her become my boss, my taskmaster, and my unrelenting critic. I was allowing my business to treat me the same way that she had.

This was such a profound experience and realization that it took me several days to take it all in.

What I learned is that when we start a business we enter into a relationship, and that relationship needs to be defined and have intentions set around it. Without this clarity we will default into old patterns of relating. I had already done the hard work of healing and changing my personal relationships so that *they* didn't recreate the toxic patterns I had with my mother. But it had never occurred to me that I might transfer my old patterns to my business.

To make the deep and necessary changes, I relied on my experience as a therapist. I knew how to define what a healthy relationship looked like and what components were needed to make it successful. So that's what I worked with.

Here's an overview of what I did (I'll expand on it in later chapters):

1. Defined the current relationship

2. Detailed what I wanted the relationship to look like

3. Identified with my business differently

4. Wrote a vision for what the future looks like

5. Formulated boundaries

6. Set up guidelines for communication and relating to my business

After that momentous morning, I naturally began to see my clients and their businesses differently. I stopped focusing on their money and their mindset because I saw that these two goals were symptoms of something deeper. Instead, I focused more on helping them to see how they were recreating their own childhood experiences—especially abusive patterns—within their businesses and to help them free themselves from those patterns.

My work is now focused on helping people realize how childhood trauma has impacted their businesses relationships so they can have healthier relationships overall. It is my life's work, and what I am 100 percent committed to.

Three years later, my business and I have a healthier partnership, one that has allowed me to bring my work to the world and help people change their lives. Imagine if I had chosen to give in to the despair I'd felt that one low morning instead of trying one more thing to feel more inspired!

I have since gone back and re-read that pivotal story in *Big Magic*. It had no emotional charge around it anymore. In fact, I had a hard time finding it in the book. It was a case of the right idea at the right time.

So, where do we go from here?

Imagine what is around the corner for you. Can you achieve your big dreams with the current partnership you have with your business? Or do you need to make some changes to feel more inspired and more supported? The stakes are high. Will you say yes to what comes next? I sure hope so.

Chapter Two

What is your Relationship with your Business – and Why is it So Bad?

One of the first questions I always ask my clients is, "Why did you start your business?" The answer I usually hear is that they wanted more money and financial freedom. That may be part of it, but I always ask people to look deeper. I want people to create emotional sustainability and learn how to love and feel loved by their business—and that takes honesty.

There is a reason that people say they want more money and more freedom, and it goes beyond the obvious. Sometimes they want to prove something to someone. ("My dad said I'd never amount to anything. I'll show him!") Sometimes they experienced physical trauma as a child and making money equals not only independence but also protection and safety from future trauma. This is one of the reasons that I see so many business owners who are not satisfied when they reach their twin goals of making money and having more freedom. There is often a hidden agenda at play.

In my time as a money mindset coach, it was 100 percent clear to me that the struggles that my clients were having were rarely about money. The causes were deeper. The money represented safety, security, acceptance, you name it. Their emotional needs were being met by money—or so they thought.

It is important to identify why you *really* started your business. Knowing what your hidden agenda is helps you stay clear about what your emotional needs are within it. If you really started your business to rebel against those who hurt you and to feel powerful, it may initially feel good but you will probably never achieve the emotional relief that you are seeking.

When I started asking my clients how they hoped they'd feel when they started their business, the most common answers to these questions weren't very deep—"I hoped that being my own boss would give me more freedom" or "I never thought about how I'd feel about it. I only thought about what kind of product I would sell, who my clients might be."

But when I started to ask "why did you start your business" in slightly different, more creative ways, I got deeper answers. I reshaped my questions this way:

When you started your business, what did you want to get more of, or to feel more of?

What are some deeper needs beneath the surface that you may have been trying to satisfy by founding your company?

What have you said to yourself about what will happen, what you will get, or what you will prove if your business is successful?

How did you feel when you worked one more hour, got one more sale and hit your first milestones? Did you experience relief? Did you feel accomplished? Or, did you only feel driven to achieve more?

The answers ranged across the map but they all gave me insight into the embedded patterns that were undermining my clients' happiness and success at work.

For the first question—what did you want to get more of or feel more of when you started your business?—clients would say things like, "I wanted to be seen and get more recognition. I felt like no matter what I did in my previous jobs, I was never acknowledged or appreciated. At least with my own business I had hoped I would be given credit for my hard work." This can be a healthy reason to start a business but it can backfire—especially if you are not used to giving yourself recognition. If we do not have a healthy sense of self, we can defer our worthiness to someone's external impression. This replicates that pattern of not feeling worthy of recognition or celebration.

When I asked my clients which deeper needs were being met by starting their business, the answers were righteous and inspiring. For instance, I had one client who said she'd had a heightened sense of justice since she was a kid. "I saw so many unfair things happening around me and when I started my career, I had a very low tolerance for how unfair things were in the financial services industry," she told me. "It bothered me how I was treated—and how others were treated. So I started my financial services company with the desire to make things fairer for women, and to fix the flaws in justice that I saw around me." On the surface, this may sound like a healthy reason to start a company. But because this client was so tied to her notions of justice, when her employees pushed back on a policy, she'd take it personally and react negatively. This strained her relationship with her employees and left her feeling frustrated that her company wasn't achieving what it set out to do.

The third question—what have you said to yourself about what will happen if your business is successful?—usually yielded answers that were very revealing. "If my business is successful, then I will prove to those who discounted me that they should've paid me closer attention. I will rebel against the unfair and biased systems that I grew up with and show that things can be done differently and that the underdog can win. I will finally get the acknowledgement and respect that I deserve and it will be one hell of a highschool reunion!"

Plenty of people start their business to be their own boss and have more freedom, but there are some people for whom their company *is* an act of rebellion. On the one hand, it can be highly motivating, but on the other hand, things can implode pretty quickly since it requires something to keep rebelling against. This can set up a business built on high emotion, conflict, and resistance. I've seen clients who, to stay motivated, will keep finding things to rebel against. Eventually they will rebel against their employees, their clients and themselves. Needless to say, this is dangerous territory.

Finally, when I asked my clients how they felt when they worked one more hour, got one more sale, or hit a first milestone, the answers I got were typically full of panic and anxiety. "At first each sale made me happy because I had not been in that situation before, but I quickly began to start stressing about the next sale and the next one," said one client. Said another: "I wish I could say that I felt relieved with each milestone my business achieved, but I actually

felt more afraid and more stressed out. T₁
once wanted now felt like an interrogation l.
another client told me, "No, no relief, but my ₁
it work pushed me to the brink on more than on   .
No matter how many milestones they achieveᵤ or how
much money they made, these clients were unable to accept
their accomplishments because they were still reacting to a
childhood wound or a trauma from a former boss. They were
seeking security, but that feeling of security was elusive. It
turns out that all the money in the world does not provide
internal safety.

One of the things I emphasize to my clients is this: You
bring all of who you are to what you do. That includes your
emotions, needs and wants. So while you may have never
thought about your feelings in regards to starting your
business, I can guarantee you that you have some emotions
running underneath your decisions and aspirations. It is ideal
to be connected to them and clear about what they are. We
will be talking about your vision and mission for your business
in a later chapter. For now, stay open to the idea that your
business is an emotional endeavor and how you feel about it
(and in it) matters.

Some people start their own business to be a better boss to
themselves than the boss (or bosses) they've had in the past.
Some inadvertently recreate bad boss patterns from previous

jobs, being too tough on themselves and their employees. Here are three exercises that will help you figure out which previous bosses you most identify with and how you might consciously be a better boss to the most important employee in your business: YOU.

🖤

EXERCISE 1

I want you to think back on a bad boss you have had. Perhaps it was someone who was mean to you. Maybe he or she was not your favorite, or you just did not click in some crucial way. Or, maybe this boss was downright emotionally abusive.

What was it about them that made you think of them as a "bad" boss? Were they annoying? Condescending? Did they take credit for your hard work? See if you can come up with five characteristics to describe them and why. Visualize yourself there with them, and dig into this scenario.

Want to take it even further? Grab your pen and use this page to answer these questions. Feel free to write about what comes up for you.

A. How did you feel being around this boss?

_____

_____

_____

_____

_____

_____

B. How did your boss communicate or not communicate with you?

_____

_____

_____

_____

_____

_____

C. In what way did this boss treat you differently than he or she treated others?

_____

_____

_____

_____

_____

_____

Notice how you are feeling in your body and what kind of reactions you are having. Are you saying to yourself anything about this person and why you started your own business? Are you in a moment of "I'll show them!" Or are you saying, "I'll never be like them!"? Spend time observing your own reactions and if you're interested in exploring this inner dialogue more, do some journaling on it. We'll be coming back to this.

EXERCISE 2

Now think back to a boss you had that you enjoyed working for. See if you can come up with a description of who they were and how you related to them. What was it about them that made you feel this way?

Grab your pen again and write down your answers below. Feel free to write even more about what comes up for you.

A. Write down five characteristics of this nice boss. For example, what made her or him amazing?

_____

_____

_____

_____

_____

B. How did you feel being around this boss?

_____

_____

_____

_____

_____

_____

C. How did she or he communicate or not communicate?

_____

_____

_____

_____

_____

D. In what way did she or he support or value you?

_____

_____

_____

_____

_____

_____

Notice how you are feeling in your body and what kind of reactions you are having as you answer. What is your inner dialogue about this boss that you liked? Spend as much time with this as you like.

EXERCISE 3

Now we go further. Think about the characteristics of that mean boss and of that nice boss by reviewing the lists of characteristics you've made. Think about how you are as the boss of your own business. Answer the following question with honesty and curiosity, and without judgment.

A. Which boss do you most identify with? How are you adopting the habits of a mean boss? Or, how do you emulate a kind boss? (Even if you do not have employees, you are the boss of you.)

_____

_____

_____

_____

_____

B. How was it answering Part A of this exercise? What is coming up for you now?

_____

_____

_____

How to Love Your Business

_____

_____

_____

To take this further, write out longer answers and spend some time exploring this concept through journaling.

_____

_____

_____

_____

_____

_____

_____

_____

_____

_____

_____

When Mary[1] did this exercise, she discovered that she was recreating the patterns of a mean boss that she'd had years ago. This boss was hypercritical. He demanded that reports, projects and meetings be completed in very specific ways that made no sense to anyone else. Mary said that it was especially challenging because these specific demands would change from day to day—with no warning. She always felt like she was walking on eggshells and could not do anything right.

As we were talking, she recognized that she was mimicking some of those patterns in her own business. She saw the chaos that she had created for herself by making decisions about a project one day, sharing the tasks with her team, only to feel insecure about the project, and changing the whole scope the next day. Needless to say, this confused her staff.

Knowing what kind of boss you have become to yourself and to others is vital to understanding what kind of relationship you have with your business. Do you feel supported and loved by your business? Or does it feel demanding and demeaning? Are you a mean boss to yourself? Or have you learned to be a loving and supportive boss?

Does your business feel and look like you imagined it would? Or has it taken on a life of its own that you feel controlled by

---

[1] All names of clients have been changed throughout.

and out of touch with? In the next chapter, we are going to go even deeper to explore how this dynamic could have been set up and who your business truly represents.

♥ ♥ ♥

Chapter 3

Where Have You Felt This Way Before?

My relationship with my mother was the first of many complex and abusive relationships that I fell prey to in childhood, and then later—unwittingly—recreated as an adult.

When I realized that I was using my business as a tool to abuse myself, I used some basic inquiries to identify who my business had become to me. First, I asked myself, "Where have I felt this way before?"

At work, I felt like I could do nothing right. (This was all in my own head, mind you. I never had a client complain to me or criticize my work ethic.) Nonetheless, I felt that every decision I made was the wrong one, that I was letting everyone down because I couldn't make enough money, focus enough, or give enough, I felt like a loser. Those were my clues.

I recognized these feelings. I grew up in a family where I was the scapegoat. I could do no right by my mom. According to her, I was lazy, uncooperative, mean, and always in trouble. In her eyes, I was a bad kid. The majority of the abuse was verbal and emotional, but sometimes it would turn physical. There was no way to win at this game because my mom and family members were invested in me being wrong.

This pattern went on to be recreated in my relationship with teachers and counselors at school. I had an undiagnosed learning disability, so I processed information differently. I went from a household where I was labeled a problem child to a classroom where my inability to learn, do homework, and understand was my fault. In school as at home, I believed that if I were better, smarter, stronger, nicer, or more compliant, then maybe I would be safe, and seen for the smart feisty child that I really was.

This pattern played out in friendships, in romantic relationships and even in workplaces. Because of my undiagnosed learning differences, which meant I processed information slower, I had difficulty concentrating. I began to see myself as "bad." Somehow, I was the problem that needed to be fixed. I needed to be more of something, or less of something: better, smarter, more willing to sacrifice, etc. In effect, I handed my power over again and again in an attempt to try and make things better because I was *always* the problem that needed to be solved.

Because this pattern was so familiar, it was very easy for me to fall back into it. My business had become a personification of my mother. I had handed over my power to the invisible "they."

My client Amanda grew up in a household where her mother was neglectful, bordering on abusive. She would tell Amanda, "You have a roof over your head, figure it out." So, Amanda did. From the age of six, she was expected to take care of her little sister, get both herself and her sister dressed and ready for school, and pack their lunches. (Her father, who was in and out, was even less reliable than her mother.)

Amanda soon realized that through achievement at school, she could get attention and by being productive she could bring safety and security to herself and her sister. The sisters graduated from high school early and each had full rides to college—all while they had a mother who was emotionally and physically abusive. After college, Amanda created a career in recruiting where she was a high achiever. She was very polished, skilled, and sought-after.

Several years ago, she left her high-powered job to begin her own business, because the corporate culture had become so toxic. When she was finally on her own without the structure and scaffolding of achievement around her, there was one crucial thing missing. There was no boss or colleague to give her praise for her accomplishments. There was no one to say,

"Hey, this report you did was fantastic!" or "That talk that you gave brought in a new client!"

As she began to build her own business, she was absolutely exhausting herself trying to get that feeling of safety again through achievement and productivity. At heart, she was still trying to please her mother. She had created an abusive relationship with her business where she was recreating these toxic patterns of trying to overcome her mother's neglect and abuse. But of course, no amount of money or clients could do that. As a result, she could never feel safe.

In our work together, I helped Amanda recognize, first of all, that the experiences she had in her childhood were, actually, trauma. And I helped her see that she had overcome that trauma by creating these patterns of behavior that looked very productive and functional.

But in actuality, these behaviors—which from the outside made her seem like a healthy and well-adjusted person— were keeping her stuck in trauma patterns. When she was able to see that, she was able to change the relationship she had with her business from one where she never felt satisfied or accomplished to one where she would wake up in the morning and ask herself (and her "inner kiddo"), "What are we gonna do today?" She began to let some of those external ways of validating herself fall away and she was able to build her business in a way that felt more comfortable.

It turned out that Amanda is not naturally a high achiever. Her strengths are her creativity and sensitivity. With this insight, she was able to build a business that was more in line with who she genuinely is and have a relationship with it that was supportive instead of undermining.

We recreate patterns that we grow up with because they feel familiar. We do it in our romantic relationships, our friendships, and in other environments like our businesses.

I had another client tell me that she was afraid to confront her boss because he reminded her of her father. In every place in her life, she had found her voice, set up boundaries, and felt secure and satisfied. The exception was at her workplace. This boss triggered the childhood trauma she suffered at the hands of her father, and so she took the abuse, did not speak out against it, and tip-toed around him. She was letting him steal her power and that made her angry at herself. But she was unsure of how to change the dynamic.

When you start a business no one asks you, "Hey, what kind of relationships have you been in, and what was your role in them?" or "What worked for you and what didn't?"

We have been taught to compartmentalize our lives, to drop our "baggage" at the door when we go to the office or start a business. There's no room for emotions, vulnerability, or even mental health problems when it comes to workplaces. But that means you end up only bringing a part of yourself to your business—not your whole messy, complicated, and fully human self. What I'm trying to say is that you will get more out of your business if you integrate all parts of yourself.

Those challenging relationships can motivate you to go into business and create high-level skill sets. But the baggage they carry can also make it impossible to achieve success.

EXERCISE 1

Go back to that list of mean boss/nice boss characteristics that you completed in Chapter 2. (Exercises 1-2, pages 15-17.) With honest curiosity and without judgment, look at your responses with fresh eyes. Ask yourself:

A. When have I felt this way in my life before my business?

_____

_____

_____

_____

_____

B. Who do I recognize in these mean boss/nice boss relationship patterns?

_____

_____

_____

_____

_____

C. If you were to assign your business a name or personality, what would that be? Would it be someone you loved and felt supported by? Or would it be someone who always made you uneasy and insecure? Write out your answers and spend some time exploring this concept through journaling about these questions.

_____

_____

_____

_____

_____

_____

_____

_____

_____

_____

Let's stop here and take some deep breaths in and out. A few more times. Even close your eyes for just a moment to let the exercise and your responses sink in.

EXERCISE 2

Next, write down any other realizations that came up as you did this exercise, or that are coming up for you now, any "aha" moments. Do this without judgment. You are gathering information that will help you create a "pattern disruption" in how you relate to your business. (A pattern disruption is when we break out of a former, habitual way of thinking.)

_____

_____

_____

_____

_____

_____

_____

_____

_____

You have to identify the relationship you have with your business honestly before you can define and embrace the relationship that you want to have with it. In the next chapter, we get to the fun part: how to fall in love with our business.

♥ ♥ ♥

Chapter 4

Let's Fall In Love

When I recognized that I had been abusing myself with my business by setting it up to emulate the relationship I'd had with my mom, I knew that I had to redefine the relationship. I did not start my business to be miserable or to feel taken advantage of. Hell, I could do that by working for someone else and at least have great benefits like medical and dental coverage, and a 401K.

I started my business in order to achieve my biggest dreams and to help other people achieve theirs as well. I could not do that within the abusive partnership I had created. I had to take a deeper look and ask myself, "What kind of relationship do I *want* to have with my business?"

Too often, we don't give ourselves the time and space to create a bigger picture of what we want in our business or in our lives, for that matter. Creation of our business first comes from a deep *why* and then gets buried by the *how*. For instance, I started my own business so I could leave the toxic workplace I was in, set my own hours, and gain financial freedom. But those "whys" ended up getting hijacked by the everyday tasks of writing more emails, increasing sales, and scoring more clients (the "hows.") If we took a moment to explore the notion of ourselves in relation to our business, and what paradigm we want to have, I believe many of us would have a different outcome.

We create our businesses with hope and excitement for the future, much like we enter into a new relationship. And just as we can recreate patterns from our private lives in our relationship with our business, we can fall into the same type of personal relationships over and over. I know what I speak of. As I mentioned in the introduction, I have been married three times. It took a lot of therapy and personal development for me to see that I'd been recreating the same dysfunctional dynamic in each of my romantic relationships. Once I saw that, I could choose to create a new one that was free of past constraints.

What I learned is that my business is also worth that investment of time and energy—and a complete paradigm shift as well. I needed to do more than focus on dollars and cents, systems, marketing, networking, program development, and coaching. You know, all the hows. I learned that I needed to create an intimate, loving relationship with my business, and dig up my why.

Initially, I had a hard time with this. I did not have many good role models for relationships that I could replicate in my life, other than the one I had fought so hard for in my marriage to my current husband, Jason. What I learned in this marriage is that with intention and honesty, a relationship can be loving and supportive instead of demanding and demeaning. With my business, I had to break it down into steps so that I could get the bigger picture of this business relationship.

♥

The Steps I Took

I'm going to walk you through the many steps that I took in order to develop a loving relationship with my own business. I will also share some colorful stories from clients who have taken the same steps and come out with a stronger, better relationship with their businesses. I love offering this process in a workshop because there is magic in the moment when I see a participant connect the dots and see their business in a whole new light.

Ready to get all lovey-dovey? Let's do it!

That cold morning when I had my *aha* moment, I had to sit down and journal all of my feelings to get them out. Here are the questions that I asked myself:

1. **Do I love my business, and if so why?** The answer was a resounding yes. I loved my business very much. I loved the fact that I was able to help so many amazing people, and that it had gotten me out of the drudgery of working for someone else every day. I also loved that it let me explore big ideas on how to change the world of small business ownership and entrepreneurship. I loved that my business reflected the values that I have of freedom and authentic leadership. I loved, loved, loved my business.

2. **Does my business love me in return? Do I feel supported by it? Do I feel like we are connected in a vision or just moving through tasks every day?** As I journaled, I realized that I felt like there was a part of my business that wanted to love me, but it was only a whisper. Most of the time, I felt like my business was mad at me, that I was in trouble, that no one would like me or want to work with me, and that every time a potential client said no, my business would be smug and demeaning. Instead of working 9 a.m. to 5 p.m. for someone else, I felt driven by my business to work all

the time, often getting nowhere. I would meet with my business coach and we would discuss a perfect plan to market my programs and then I could not follow through on the plan. I was working long hours and on weekends basically for free because I was not making the sales that I needed. I was afraid to put myself out there and speak about my expertise because I never felt like I was good enough to warrant the attention. And, even on days where I did some amazing work with a client, or had a successful sales call, I still felt like it didn't matter. It was as if my business was a fickle mistress who was always changing the game on how to win my love and attention. In short, my business, which existed in my head and in my life as a fully realized entity, separate from "me," did not love me. It was, in fact, abusive and most days I was afraid of it."

Now that it was clear that my business was replicating abusive patterns, I began to ask myself more questions.

I wrote down a list of all the things that I would want from my business if it was a person. What attributes did I want it to have? How did I want to relate to it?

These were my answers:

1. **How did I want to relate to my business?** I wanted to feel connected and in daily communication with my business. I wanted a daily dialogue about what works and what doesn't, about what feels right and what feels wrong. A clear line of communication with no judgments. I wanted to be nurtured by my business, emotionally and financially. I want to nurture my business in return.

2. **What attributes did I want it to have?** I wanted my business to be playful and fun, not too serious. I do not respond well to serious, stoic and demanding people. Why would I want my business to be like that?

I also wrote down a list of what I would like my partnership to look like with this entity. I thought about all of the relationships that I'd had in my life and what they looked like. For example, with my husband Jason, our relationship is built on humor and a deep respect for one another. He does most of the cooking in our home because I absolutely hate doing it. I do things that he hates doing—such as cleaning up the kitchen, vacuuming and meal-planning. We each want to protect the other from activities that are draining. We have our own language and secret jokes that have become a part of our story. I rarely have to explain myself to him. At this point, we have history, so he knows what I mean most of the time. He could finish my sentences if need be.

During this exercise, I also wrote down what it was like to work with a dear friend, Susan, who I trusted and who trusted me. I thought about how important it was that I'd left the social work arena—where I'd been mentally and emotionally beat up—and how having her support and empathy made it easier to push back against my supervisors' unethical behavior. In other words, Susan really had my back.

The key emotions here were that I felt respected, nurtured, safe, understood, and humored.

I was beginning to see what I really wanted from the partnership, to understand how I wanted to feel, what kind of personality my business might have. That made it easier to think about what I could do to create it as an intentional relationship. How could I connect with my business every day?

I looked at all the lists that I had created and asked myself some more questions. If I were to think of my business as an entity, what would it look like? Would it be a spiritual presence, an animal, a celebrity? Could it be an energy source or a planet? I needed it to be something that I was eager to relate to.

I began to imagine my business as a partner in creation.

When I sat down and answered all of these questions for myself I let myself be dreamy and somewhat goofy about it. I allowed any answer to be okay. When I relate what came up in talks on this topic, people often laugh uncontrollably.

What I realized is that my business was The Ghost of Christmas Present. Not just any version of him, but the *Muppet* version. Let me tell you why. First of all, he is vibrant, jovial, and loves to party. He has the best food and drink, and knows how to have a good time. He does not take himself too seriously. He is also very wise and knows that we must look at the past so that we can change our future. He knows that the future can change with one breath in the present moment. He knows that what really counts is right here—this moment.

I have since recognized that he is a stand-in for the father I always needed. That he has the bigger-than-life benevolent and jovial presence of my favorite planet, Jupiter. I can be too serious at times, so he helps me feel powerful and present and yet still funny at the same time. He is so very important to me.

I then formalized this picture of my business by printing out a picture of The Ghost of Christmas Present and putting it over my desk so I could remember him and be reminded that he was my business partner and that he had my back. This may sound silly, but it worked.

This is one of my favorite parts of the exercise: creating and sharing our business entity's personas. I had a client, Kimberly, who had a very demanding and critical mom. She had recreated a relationship with her business much like mine where she felt very unsupported and insecure. She mainly wanted to feel supported, secure, and strong. So, when she went through this exercise, the business entity she chose was an oak tree. The oak tree represented her business because she wanted to have deep roots where she could feel secure and stable. She wanted to have a sturdy trunk that could support all of her dreams and her big ideas and all her creativity— which is what all the branches and leaves were. She wanted her business to not only be supportive and protective of her, but also to all of those around her, the way that trees provide a habitat for the animals, shade for all creatures, and oxygen. Her tree also had branches that reached high up to the sky, because she had such ambition for her business.

Another client, Lynn, had parents who were very absent. She could only get their attention if she morphed herself into somebody or something else. Likewise, with her business, she was constantly changing programs and coming up with new ideas. As a result, she was having a hard time making sustainable revenue and establishing her expertise and brand recognition. In this exercise, she chose the entity of a butterfly to represent her business. A butterfly has metamorphosed and has taken flight. It is beautiful and it has a purpose. It's also not going to change again.

♥

Write a Love Letter

This next part is where people usually look at me and say, "Okay Nicole, now I really know that you have lost your mind." I'm okay with that.

Do you know what I did next? I wrote love letters. Yup, sure did. I wrote a love letter to my business, and then one from my business back to me. I know, I know. My business cannot really write a letter. But I have two hands and can type, so I asked it what it would want to say.

I wrote a love letter to my business and in it, I told it why I loved it so much. I told it what my commitments to it are, and why I was so excited about the work that we would do together. It honestly felt like marriage vows in some way. They were statements that affirmed how I felt, why I thought it was fantastic, and my vision for our future.

When I wrote a love letter to me from my business—my Muppet ghosty—I wrote down everything that I hoped my business would say to me. All of the things that it is excited about, its hopes for our relationship and the commitments that it would make to me.

Here's the thing about this love letter exercise—people tend to either love it or hate it. Okay, so hate might be a bit strong, but let's say that they don't connect with the idea of being in love with their business. I totally get that and it is okay.

Being in love is not always about a romantic relationship, it is a deep, intimate connection with someone or something that causes you to feel profoundly alive. It informs how you behave and what your desires are in relationship to this person or thing.

I have a lot of artist friends and they will often tell me that they are in love with their latest creation or even their studio. Do you see what I mean here?

Here are my love letters:

Dear Chris,

I am so thankful for you. I never imagined that I would have the privilege of owning my own business and doing impactful work in the world outside of social work. You have given me the opportunity to create such a special outlet for my creativity and sense of purpose. What I love about you so much is that you are wise and you see the world as I do. You know that we must look back to acknowledge what got us here and that the future can be changed by our willingness to value this present moment. You believe that we can change the whole trajectory of our lives by honoring the present.

You have such wisdom and also really know how to have a good time and you delight in the pleasures of life that are available to us. This is what I need more of in my life.

I am sorry that I neglected you. Forgive me for using this pure creative space to re-create some gnarly old patterns. I vow to you that I will stay firm in honoring my business as a treasured relationship that deserves fun, love, protection and room to dream. Thank you.

Nicole

Dear Nicole,

What I dig about you is that you are not afraid to rattle some cages and I really appreciate that in a person. I deeply feel your commitment to learning from your past and using it to change your future. I am so proud that you help others do the same thing for themselves in their lives and businesses. You are radical and I love you for that. I forgive you for letting our relationship get twisted and will accept that it was a learning experience that you needed to go through. You are brave, smart, loving and creative and we will work on helping you have more fun.

I vow to support you and remind you that you are loved.

Your one and only Muppet ghost,
Chris

Here's an example of a client's love letter to her business "persona" and one from her persona to herself:

Dearest Oak Tree,

I love you! I love the steady way you have about you. I love how you take care of me financially, while allowing me to fully express my creative side. I love the partnership we have and how we work together to nurture the people we interact with. I love how you support me to take care of myself, allow me to spend quality time with my family and take them on adventures. I love the way we work together to help those that are less fortunate. I love how reliable you are. I always know I can depend on you to be there for me when I need you. Thank you! Thank you for making my family and me so happy and for working with me to make our dreams come true.

Love,
Kimberly

P.S. I know that I haven't always been the easiest person to take care of, and I am working to improve that. I promise that I will work on communicating my needs to you, setting boundaries so that I don't resent the time that you need. and making time to hang out with you to talk regularly. not just when I feel like it. I promise that I will honor the consistency you provide for me by making sure I give you the attention you deserve. I will not wait until the last minute to demand things from you. and instead will plan properly so that we can take care of each other properly. I so love you and cannot wait to see how our relationship continues to grow and the millions of lives we will be able to affect working together.

Oh Kimberly,

How I have longed to hear you write these words. I have been patiently waiting for you to acknowledge our relationship for so long. I have longed to work with you instead of trying to anticipate your needs and fight against you. You have so many talents and have such a gift to bring to the world and I am delighted to help you bring that vision to light and change the lives of so many around us. I know that as we work together, taking consistent, steady action together that your impact on the world will explode and I can provide the lifestyle I have always dreamed for you. Now that you no longer feel the need to hide our relationship anymore, I can finally yell from the

rooftops how amazing we are together and how much I adore
you. Working together, there is nothing we cannot accomplish. I
love you and can't wait to see the impact we have on the world.

Yours,
Oak Tree

If you are still not connecting with the love letter idea, here is a modification. I was teaching a "Lunch & Learn" at a local co-working facility called The Candy Factory and I was thrilled that there were some men at the table. One of the men raised his hand when I came to this part of the training and he said, "I'm sorry, but when I think of writing a love letter, I struggle." So I asked him this, "Do you have a best friend? A friend that you have known a long time and that is your ride-or-die best bud?" He said, "Of course. I was in the military as a young man and I still have friends from that time that I am as loyal to as I am to my wife."

"Great!" I said. "Write a letter to your business as if it were to him. Outline your devotion, loyalty, and the fun you have had and will have. Write them as if they are commitments and vows to this best friend of yours."

I then told him to write a letter back to himself from this loyal friend who has his back and knows him better than anyone. The kind of friend that will call him out and make him laugh harder than anyone else. That friend that he could trust with his life, his money and his business.

Once I was able to reframe this for him, he was on board and went from being resistant to excited. As Brené Brown teaches, the most basic human needs are connection and belonging. I believe that the practices and processes outlined in this book will give you the pathway to connect to your business on a deeper level, so that you feel your business belongs to you.

When I offer this exercise in a workshop or retreat, I ask anyone who wants to read her or his letters out loud to do so. In that setting we have already identified who our business reminds us of, and we've shared that insight with one another. Have I mentioned that this is my favorite part of this process? I love hearing those letters. It is exciting to see my workshop participants' eyes light up and, sometimes, see their tears fall when they realize that they have been missing out on so much love and support from their business.

It may sound kooky, but my desire is for you to have a bond with your business.

If you would like to share your love letters with me, this is where you can send them: Nicole@lewis-keeber.com.

❤ ❤ ❤

Chapter 5

Now That We've Found Love, What Are We Going to Do?

The very first time I taught the idea that we often replicate our toxic patterns in our relationships to our businesses, it was in a breakout session at the Polka Dot Powerhouse Annual Celebration in Chicago.

I had my PowerPoint presentation ready to go, but when I got to the conference room there was no cord to connect the computer to the projector. I was already nervous, but when I realized that there was no tech person on hand to help me I got very flustered. The room was rapidly filling up. Soon there would be 80 women present, but I had no mic to help them hear me and no visual presentation they could follow.

If this had happened to me before I built a loving relationship with my business, I would have let my nerves take over. I would have spun out.

Later, my friend Megan, who was in the room, said to me, "I could see your nerves kick in, but then you took a big breath and I could see you gain control." In that moment, I connected with my inner Spirit of Christmas Present Muppet. I heard his jovial laughter. He had a message for me that said, "You don't like PowerPoint anyway. This way you can walk through the room so they can hear you better and you can connect with them in a more genuine way."

In my moment of nerves, instead of bailing, hiding, or crashing, I had connected with my business. In fact, this ended up being the best case scenario because I got the audience involved and it helped me feel less like a talking head and more like a co-creator of the experience.

The talk went so well that 80 percent of the women in the room stayed to ask questions and share their *aha* moments. One woman said, "When you said that you see women not making any room for their businesses and are literally working from a corner of the kitchen table, you called me out. I work from a broken chair in my kitchen. I never take a lunch break. If I worked for an employer that did that I would quit and report them. Why am I doing that to myself?"

Another woman later told me that, after my session, she immediately grabbed her journal and went outside to connect with her business and write love letters. Yet another woman walked up to me and said, "This is a powerful idea. But now that I know I have a relationship with my business, have identified its persona and have written my love letters, what comes next? How do I take this *aha* and turn it into action?"

I was so happy that she asked me this question because I had been working on outlining what comes next for myself and my clients too.

That was the day that I realized this idea was so much more than a workshop or a process for a few select clients, or a roomful of women at a conference.

I want you to have a business you love and I want you to learn how to stay in love with it as well. That requires a roadmap and some additional steps. You must define your values, articulate your vision for your business, and also write down the mission that is driving you. These are critical aspects to having a business you love and that loves you back.

Values Clarification: The Beginning of Your Road Map

Now that you and your business have found one another and have made vows and commitments, it is important to envision what you want to do together. You need a road map for what comes next and, more importantly, why you want to travel together in that way.

As a therapist who worked with couples in my private practice, I saw that the most successful couples were the ones who had shared values. It is not uncommon for individuals to not know what their true values are, let alone couples. People usually adopt some values from family, others from peers or the culture at large, and yet they still have not really asked themselves, "What do *I* value?" They rarely ask their partner what he or she values and certainly haven't identified what they value as a *couple*.

The couples that were able to get clear about their own values—without merely defaulting to their family's or culture's values—were more successful at navigating their futures together.

So, back to you and your business. You must identify what your values are so that you can then create a vision and mission for this powerful relationship that you are building.

Identifying your own personal values—not necessarily what you have been taught—can be difficult. Brené Brown works with companies, managers, and executives to help them identify what their values are so that they know when they are in and out of integrity. "Living into our values is one of the four skill sets that make up Daring Leadership. It means that we do more than profess our values, we practice them," writes Brown in her 2018 book *Dare to Lead*. "We walk our talk—we are clear about what we believe and hold important, and we take care that our intentions, words, thoughts, and behaviors align with those beliefs."

It is important to discover what your shared values are for you and your business so that you can use them as a compass to navigate your future and as a way to make decisions about what you will and won't do. Once you have your values nailed down, it will make all business-related decisions much easier.

Check in with yourself and your business persona, then scan this list of values below and circle the five that resonate most with you.

Accountability

Achievement

Adaptability

Adventure

Altruism

Ambition

Authenticity

Balance

Beauty

Being the best

Belonging

Caring

Collaboration

Commitment

Community

Compassion

Competence	*Financial stability*
Confidence	*Forgiveness*
Connection	*Freedom*
Contentment	*Friendship*
Contribution	*Fun*
Cooperation	*Future generations*
Courage	*Generosity*
Creativity	*Giving back*
Curiosity	*Grace*
Dignity	*Gratitude*
Diversity	*Growth*
Efficiency	*Harmony*
Environment	*Health*
Equality	*Home*
Ethics	*Honesty*
Excellence	*Hope*
Fairness	*Humility*
Faith	*Humor*
Family	*Inclusion*

Now That We've Found Love, What Are We Going to Do?

Independence	Order
Initiative	Parenting
Integrity	Patience
Intuition	Peace
Joy	Perseverance
Job security	Personal fulfillment
Justice	Power
Kindness	Pride
Knowledge	Recognition
Leadership	Reliability
Learning	Resourcefulness
Legacy	Respect
Leisure	Responsibility
Love	Risk-taking
Loyalty	Safety
Making a difference	Security
Nature	Self-discipline
Openness	Self-expression
Optimism	Self-respect

Serenity	*Trust*
Service	*Truth*
Simplicity	*Understanding*
Spirituality	*Uniqueness*
Sportsmanship	*Usefulness*
Stewardship	*Vision*
Success	*Vulnerability*
Teamwork	*Wealth*
Thrift	*Well-being*
Time	*Wholeheartedness*
Tradition	*Wisdom*
Travel	

After you have picked out five, see if they line up with how you want to feel in your business and what kind of partnership you want to have with it. Then, narrow it down by writing down the top three values that you and your business agree are the most important. Make sure that you display them prominently in your workspace next to the picture of your business persona.

Now that you and your business have discovered your top three values, the next step is to dream big together. What big work do you want to do in the world together? What did you envision when you decided to take this leap into business ownership? Did you have a clear idea about this when you started? Did you imagine you would have to do it all alone?

Now that you and your business have buddied up what do you think could be different?

Define Your Values

Crafting mission and vision statements for your business does not have to be as complicated as it might sound. Together they create your compass because they help keep you directed. The good news is that you can always redefine them and change them as your relationship with your business matures.

The most important first step in writing your mission and vision statements is for you to define your values. This is much easier to do when it is your own business and not one you work for.

Think back to the love letter exercise. In it, you have already begun to see what is important to you and your business. Now, look at your letters and see what words, actions and feelings come up often.

If you are struggling to identify what your values are in your business, you can always take a look at your life and answer some questions to see what you, personally, value.

♥

Identify Your Business's Values

Look at times in your life when you had the most joy and happiness. Explore what the circumstances were in your life at that time. What were you doing? What was it about the situation that made you happy and content? That may be a value.

Look at times in your life where you felt proud of yourself and happy with your choices. They could be choices in your work, career, relationships, health, etc.

Look at the experiences you have had when you felt most fulfilled because you were in alignment with your purpose.

What was happening at that moment? What was the driving force and how did you feel?

As you sit with your answers, you will start to see common threads and your values will start to bubble to the surface. This is exactly what happened for a woman who attended my Love Your Business School program. At first, the exercise frustrated her, because she couldn't narrow her values down to just three. So I had her read her list to me: efficiency, excellence, achievement, competence, initiative, integrity, accountability, reliability, honesty, success, ethics, resourcefulness, ownership, and integrity. We then grouped the ones that were most alike to see how we could narrow down her list.

What we discovered is that, overall, she values taking initiative. Being competent, reliable, resourceful, and responsible all require initiative, so we bundled those together under the heading Initiative. We then looked at honesty, ethics, and accountability and bundled them together, choosing the word Integrity to represent them. We then tapped into what all of these values added up to and how she wanted her business to be seen by the world and how she wanted to feel about it. Finally, we came up with Excellence for the final value.

Once you have written down your top ten values, start to narrow them down to the top three that are most related to the mission and vision of your business. If you have trouble, look at three values and ask yourself, "If I can only accomplish one of these, what would be most important?" Then repeat until you have worked through the whole list. What values remain? Would you be happy and proud to tell someone that these are the values of you and your business?

This exercise does not have to be hard. Get a list together, follow your intuition, and let your business entity guide you. There are no wrong answers—that is the beauty of this. These values are here to help you make decisions.

Usually, when I ask a client or a group to create a mission and vision statement, they roll their eyes. The collective sigh is audible; it's like everyone has corporate PTSD. We have all worked for companies that had mission and vision statements displayed in their lobby, break room, official documentation and even on your computer wallpaper. We also saw those statements blatantly ignored. I call it corporate hypocrisy and it is a real drain on our morale.

So I am not going to ask you to recreate that particular trauma. I want you and your business to reclaim this practice and make it your own. And have fun with it! These statements are just as important as those letters you wrote to each other.

With these statements, you are putting your plans and your dreams out there.

Once you have identified your values, what is the vision you have for your business?

Get the picture of your business entity out (if you haven't already) and the three top values that you came up with while doing this exercise. When I did this I took my Muppet photo out and wrote down my three values—authenticity, consent, and freedom—on an index card and placed them next to each other. The photo of the Ghost of Christmas Present served as a jumping off point for what my vision could be. It helped me describe what my business *personality* would be.

♥

Crafting the Vision Statement

Your vision statement is a big dreamy vision for the work that you and your business will do in the world together. Use your imagination and intuition to fantasize about what is possible. Even though it may be a big far-fetched vision of the impact you'll make, in reality, it will still guide you and help you make decisions. Your vision statement is your compass for what you want to see in your future.

Guidelines for Creating Your Vision Statement

- Project 10-20 years out—what do you imagine for your business? Dream big!

- Use the present tense.

- Align your vision with your values and goals.

- Write it with your full emotion and intuition.

- Freewrite it initially if you like and then edit it down. It does not have to be super long.

There may be a time when you need to share your vision with employees, partners, and funders so make sure that what you write is understandable to someone outside of your business bubble. (That is: stay away from corporate jargon.)

Your vision statement outlines the big juicy vision you and your business have for yourselves.

A vision statement is usually a sentence or two and will include reference to your values and the impact that you want to have on the world or your industry. It also gives you a place to reverse engineer your mission statement.

Questions to Answer in Creating Your Vision Statement

- What are the values that I share with my business?

- What impact do my business and I want to have on my industry, my community or even the world?

- What will the culture of my business look like when interacting with those who are connected to it?

- When I have met my outrageous goal for my business what will that look like?

♥

Crafting the Mission Statement

A mission statement declares an organization's purpose, and how it will achieve the vision you defined. That often includes a general description of the organization, its function, and its objectives. It should also detail how you and your business will make the big dream vision happen. You can think of it as the recipe for your business, or the unique instructions for how you will accomplish the vision.

Questions to Answer in Creating Your Mission Statement

- What do you do for your customers?

- What does your business do for you as the owner?

- What does your business do for your employees? (If you have them.)

- What qualities do you have as a company while offering this goodness to the world?

Play around with these ideas. You can even combine your mission and vision statements in the same paragraph. Remember, this is *your* business. You get to do it as you like. There are no shoulds. There are no "have to's." Here is clean energy company Tesla's mission and vision statement, one after the other: "To accelerate the world's transition to sustainable energy. To create the most compelling car company of the 21st century by driving the world's transition to electric vehicles."

In fact, if you are a rebel like me you can opt out of this altogether and have a simple statement or mantra that you use as your compass. Most important is that you and your business are on the same page, and know how to make decisions based on your shared values. You need something you can look at daily to keep you on track. We all need reminders to help us remember what we're doing. We all get stuck in the noise of running a business.

One of my participants at the Polka Dot Powerhouse workshop decided to write her mission and vision statements and then manifest both through her art work. It was a value of hers to connect with these deeper compass concepts not just through the written language, but also through a visual representation. For her, the artwork sparked excitement and energy when she saw it, in a way that words on a page never could. I encourage you to experiment in the same way.

♥ ♥ ♥

Chapter 6

Take Up Space

In this chapter we are going to talk about taking up space literally and figuratively.

Many years ago, I worked with a coaching client who told me that her entire life she had been trying not to take up space. Becky was the tallest girl in her class and in her family. Her height made her feel different. She felt shame about taking up space, so she began slouching. She told me how she went from trying to shrink herself physically to taking up less and less energetic space in her life and her career.

She reflected on the times in her life when she could have been more straightforward, asking for what she needed and wanted. Instead, she would defer and shrink back. With her friends, she never had an opinion about which movie to see or where to hang out. She went to a local college instead of to the out-of-state university she wanted to attend because she did not want to cost her parents too much money. The reality was that her family could have afforded to send her where she wanted to go, but by that point, she had become an expert at shrinking.

It wasn't until she started seeing a physical therapist for back and neck pain that she confronted her unwillingness to take up space. When she was doing her PT homework, Becky realized that it was harder for her to do the exercises there than it was at the therapist's office because she felt unable to take up space and stand up straight around her family. She told me, "I was physically in pain because I was not allowing myself to live up to my full potential there—the full body that God gave me. I recognized that this was keeping me from feeling confident and worthy."

She was tearful when she recounted to me how uncomfortable it was for her to stand tall at her full height and hold her head held high, especially around her family. Her epiphany at physical therapy inspired her to seek out psychotherapy to learn how she could take up more emotional space in her life as well.

She worked hard to claim space in her relationship with her husband and to ask for what she needed as a mom. She even began to take up more space in her friendships. She told me that she lost a few friends when she was no longer quietly compliant, which hurt, but that the pain of losing a friend was less than the pain of losing herself.

By the time we worked together she had left her corporate job and had started her own consulting business and was on her way to her third year of growth and success.

Inspiring, right?

Becky is a kick-ass woman with wisdom and self-awareness. So imagine her shock and dismay when she realized that she had created a successful business that was draining her physically and emotionally.

In our first coaching session, she told me how tired and depleted she was, and how upset she was that she could not enjoy her successes. She had done everything "the right way." She worked with a mentor, got a business coach, and had made more money in year three of her business than she had made in her corporate job. But her pride in herself was diminished by her suffering.

It was clear to me that she had defaulted into old ways of operating and had not recognized it or planned for it in creating her business. So, at our next session, we talked about physical boundaries. Here is what she uncovered.

She had no dedicated space for her business. Instead, she moved around within the house. She would work from her kitchen table, but move when her kids came in. She would work from her couch with headphones on while her husband watched television. She had convinced herself that this was normal, because she was part of the "laptop lifestyle club." But in reality, this laptop lifestyle was not glamorous. She wasn't working by the pool, or in a luxury suite in Palm Springs. No, she and her laptop were moving from room to room to accommodate other people.

Once again, she was not taking up space. She did not want to inconvenience her family. She was lying to herself about how having a flexible, mobile desk-free work day was what her business as an online consultant was all about. I asked her if she liked this set-up and she said, "Hell, no!" When she had worked in an office, she enjoyed having her own space and she enjoyed being able to close the door to work. She liked having a desk and chair that accommodated her height. As she spoke wistfully about her corporate office I asked, "Why don't you have an office at home?"

"We don't have the space," she said. Knowing that there's often something else going on underneath a client's first reply, I asked her to describe the rooms she had in her house.

She told me that they had the kids' rooms, the master bedroom, and a guest room that had become a catch-all room.

"What would it take for you to claim the guest room as your office?" I asked. She was caught off guard and gave me a few half-hearted excuses.

"We need a room for people to stay in when they visit," she said, at first.

"How often does that happen?" I asked. She told me guests came through town only twice a year.

"If people only come to visit twice a year, couldn't you put them up in a hotel?" I asked.

She agreed that that would be a sensible solution. But then she said they also used that room for storage. I asked her if the things in there were really necessary to keep and, if so, was there another place to put them? Again, she gave a few half-hearted excuses. Again, I kept inquiring. Finally, she blurted out: "It seems selfish to take up an entire room just for me."

"Exactly," I said.

We worked through some of the still-unconscious beliefs she had about taking up space. I asked her if she and her business deserved to have room to grow without being disrupted every day. I would love to tell you that she agreed immediately but it took a few sessions for us to dismantle her excuses. I had to remind her that she had already done the hard work to take up space in her personal life and that she could do it again in her professional life.

Today, Becky has a dedicated office in her home and she is building a new home with her husband that has an office suite for her with a fantastic view. She went from converting a humble guest room into her home office to really honoring and celebrating her work and how important it is to her and her life.

People are not likely to give us space if we don't ask for it. They will stay within the boundaries we set for them. This is why it is so important to make space for your business—literally and figuratively, whenever possible. Your business will grow or not grow depending on the attention and space you give it. You can have success while not taking up space but it is not sustainable.

♥

Is Your Working Space Supporting You?

It's important to have an orderly and beautiful space so you can feel connected to your business and so your mind can be clear and focused. Take a few minutes to reflect. Journal about these prompts to take your reflections deeper.

- Where do you commune with your business?

- Do you have a dedicated space?

- Do you have set work hours that you protect and honor so that you can work in an intentional way?

- What is working about the physical space you run your business from?

- What is not working?

- If you do have a dedicated office, have you really claimed the space in a way that honors the relationship you are building?

I myself struggle to keep my office clean. I tend towards chaos, with papers stacked in piles and newspapers strewn over my couch. I've been trying to remind myself to clean up at the end of the day. If I'm unable to do that, I do a big clean-up at the end of the week, which always makes me feel more at peace. A clean office gives me more space emotionally and physically to be creative and productive. I have been working hard at putting rituals in place that honor the space I occupy with my business. You should, too.

Here is one more way that you can assess if your space is serving you well in supporting your boundaries. Sometimes a check list does just the trick to give us a bigger picture.

My workspace is comfortable. **Yes / No**

My workspace is either free of clutter or I tidy it up at the end of my workday/ workweek. **Yes / No**

I have enough privacy in my workspace to focus and get my tasks done without interruption. **Yes / No**

I am surrounded by things that make me feel good about my business and my work (for example, nice plants, prints, knick-knacks, positive reminders, ergonomic furniture, etc.) **Yes / No**

If I answered "no" to any of the items above, I have a plan to fix them, including a timeline, a budget, and possibly an accountability partner. **Yes / No**

♥ ♥ ♥

Chapter 7

Set Boundaries

In this chapter I want to talk about some of the boundaries that are the hardest to create and enforce. We have been taught by the hustle culture that our time, attention and output are required if we want to succeed. If you are not working, thinking about work, or networking all the time then you are not serious about your business. Or so the common wisdom goes.

I call bullshit on that. I know many successful business owners who refuse to hustle, and who are doing quite well without needing to be chained to their company.

I can hear you saying, "Well good for them, Nicole. They were able to set boundaries, but I can't." Or, as my southern sisters would say, "Well, how nice for them"—not meaning it at all.

These less-stressed but still successful business owners are no different than you and me. All they did was have a frank talk with themselves about the foundational boundaries for their business. They did the same with their employees about the boundaries required from them. I always say that people will rise to the level of the boundaries we set. If we do not set any, they will flood through and take over.

These days, it is actually easier than ever before to start a business. The online marketplace is accessible to most people. Whereas in the past, many business models required a storefront and massive amounts of inventory, now you need very little to start an online business. You don't even need to rent a space! There is a low barrier for entry.

But something has been lost with online businesses. If you open up a pizzeria, you likely have a business partner or family member who supports you, either emotionally or practically, or both. You sought financing, you carefully considered location and staffing. Who would you hire to make the store a success? Perhaps you had a conversation with your family about what sacrifices you needed to make to ensure your business flourished. Maybe you even determined that your kids would spend some time working in the pizzeria.

What I'm getting at is that you cannot open a pizza shop overnight. It takes months of planning, intention, boundary-setting and conversations with business partners, backers, and family.

If you have an online business, on the other hand, you can literally open up in 24 hours if you so desire. And some people do. On the surface, your business appears easy, nimble and accessible, an example of that laptop lifestyle you read so much about. If you decide to be a seller for a direct sales company like Pure Haven (all natural personal care products) or SendOutCards (online greeting cards), you can buy your start-up kit, or you can sign on with a company like Angie's List or Fiverr and begin getting clients within a day. But I've observed that taking shortcuts comes back to haunt the business owners who do not plan and prepare, just like the owner of the pizzeria.

Owners of online businesses need to have the same conversations and boundary-setting practices as the owners of traditional businesses do. They need to write a business plan, know how to do payroll, pay taxes, and have clear communication with their team about who is doing what and when. Otherwise, believe me, there will be conflict and chaos both with the finances of the business and with the employees.

One thing you absolutely *must* put a boundary around is the amount of time that you connect with your business. This includes the number of hours you will work. This also means letting the people around you—family members, friends— know what hours you are available and when you are not, and sticking to it. Hustle culture tells you that you need to be available 24/7. Your family and friends might expect you to be available whenever they need you. The budding entrepreneurs who want to "pick your brain" over coffee may expect you to freely offer your time. If you don't set boundaries, it will take you longer to make a profit and you may suffer burnout, both physically and mentally. That's not to say you can't make time to meet up with young entrepreneurs occasionally, it just needs to be done with intention and the knowledge that you are choosing to forgo making $500 or $2,000 that hour because you are choosing to provide support and mentorship to that person instead.

Remember your business bestie? That persona that I asked you to find in Chapter 4? Would they want you to be overly available to the point that your business and you are like chum in the water for sharks? No. Your business loves you and wants you to have sanity and safety. So you must set limits. We have all had intense jobs where our boss expected us to be available outside of office hours and did not respect our time and autonomy. How did it make you feel? Did you love that boss, or feel resentful? Reminder, dear reader, that you did not start your business to burn out.

All relationships need boundaries. They need to be defined and they need to have intentions set for them. It's the same for our businesses.

♥

Create the Necessary Boundaries so Your Business Can Thrive

Here's how you can begin to create the boundaries needed for you and your business to thrive.

1. Time. When do you tell your partner and kids, if you have them, that you are not available so you can work on your business? When do you rest? When do you shut down for the day? The week? When are you open for networking coffees or client or vendor interactions? Map this out before you launch your business. Find systems that can support you in setting these boundaries around your time such as calendar alerts, appointment schedulers that guard your calendar, and clear policies with your clients and employees about your availability.

2. Space. Look again at the space that you and your business inhabit. I want you to draw some perimeters around the place that you work and keep it as sacred as possible. Tell those around you what the rules are for this space. "If the door is closed, that means do not interrupt me, unless there's a fire." Or "When the dimmable LED mood lamp on my desk is red, that means under no circumstances are you to bother me. When the light is yellow, it means, no stupid questions like, 'Where's the cereal?' And when it's green, it means I'm free—bother me as much as you'd like." Remember you and your business deserve a dedicated home in which to live.

3. Family. Whether you have a partner, kids, or extended family around you, you will absolutely need to have a conversation with them about when you are available and when you're off limits. You will need to ask for their buy-in to your dream and maybe even redefine some roles. Perhaps this means that the household chores are re-assigned. Maybe this means that the "things we have always done" have to change to the "things we do now." Every day I see business owners trying to grow their businesses without ever having these conversations. They want to be available all the time to their clients and to their families, and don't think this requires any change in their households. This is a recipe for self-abuse. If your family loves you, they will adjust. But you must lay down the boundaries.

4. Energy. It can be exhausting to run a business, so energy management is crucial. What boundaries around your energy are you willing to create? Are you surrounded by energy vampires? Are you working nonstop and not making time for any rest or downtime? Are you walking into client meetings emotionally vulnerable, setting yourself up for feeling like a failure? Energetic boundaries were so important for me to create, especially because I'm an introvert. And as an introvert and as someone who has a learning difference, my bandwidth is pretty low. And yet I can still run a successful business when I honor this about myself and plan accordingly.

5. Have a Growth Mindset. We all have an inner critic. It is there for a very important reason: to keep us safe. In fact, our inner critic lives in the amygdala—the center of fear and anger in our brain. It really is an impossible feat to try and shut its response down, since we are biologically wired for it. So, instead of trying to ignore it, listen to it but don't let it have the final say. Have a conversation with it. For instance, you could say to it, "I get it, speaking in front of that audience feels unsafe." Or, "You're right, no one has ever built a business on the intersection of trauma and small business ownership. I know it's risky, but I believe there is a huge opportunity. So, thank you inner critic, but I'm going to move forward because there's possibility and abundance to be had."

This is an example of embracing a growth mindset, which thrives on challenges and does not see them as a failure but as an opportunity. It takes courage and a willingness to change your beliefs about what is possible when you start a business. Therefore, protect your mindset by connecting with those who also have a growth mindset and can see tasks like information-gathering as challenges, not obstacles.

Setting boundaries can be difficult because many of us—especially those of us who are women—have been conditioned not to have them. The list above includes some tangible examples of how you can begin to set boundaries for your business. If you're still struggling to set boundaries, here are three exercises that will help.

EXERCISE 1

Think back to your childhood and see if you can find positive examples of those around you who made their boundaries clear.

A. What did it look like? How did you feel about that person setting the boundary?

_____

_____

_____

_____

B. If you cannot remember any positive examples of boundary-setting, think back on what kind of memories you have about someone in your life who wasn't able to set boundaries. What did that look like? How did you feel about it?

_____

_____

_____

_____

EXERCISE 2

Do you have any memories of what it was like for you as a child when you practiced setting a boundary? Write it down. Did it go well? Was your boundary respected? Or was it overridden?

_____

_____

_____

_____

_____

_____

_____

_____

_____

_____

_____

_____

_____

_____

_____

EXERCISE 3

As an adult, has it been difficult for you to set boundaries in your relationships?

A. If so, why? What tends to happen?

_____

_____

_____

B. How does it feel when you do set a boundary and it is not respected?

_____

_____

_____

C. What do you think is the biggest barrier that holds you back from setting boundaries for yourself in your business? Write it down.

_____

_____

In the next chapter, we'll talk further about how you don't need to fire your Inner Critic and ignore it but learn to love it and partner with it for the success of your business.

Chapter 8

How to Love Your Inner Critic

As I mentioned in the last chapter, we all have an inner critic. Often, that voice is a holdover from formative relationships—a critical parent, a tough teacher, or a demanding first boss. While some self-help gurus will insist that you should dismiss that inner critic completely, I've found that the inner critic may actually have some wisdom for us. We just need to learn to listen to it and tap into what it's telling us about our childhood selves.

Recently a client was feeling defeated and ready to give up on her business. She struggled to remember why she had even started it. She was being brutal with herself and she was also being pretty nasty, abrupt and resentful towards her employees.

I asked her the question that I learned to ask as a therapist and have modified since studying Brené Brown's work. I asked her, "What is the story you are telling yourself about this?"

She said, "The story that I'm telling myself is that I was not meant to be a business owner and that my father was right about me not being capable enough to do anything more than be a teacher and a mom. I'm telling myself that my employees don't like me and that they only want the money and that eventually, they will leave because I am not fun to work for. I'm telling myself that I'm dumb and that they were right because this is all too hard and I don't think I can do it anymore."

Can you relate to that inner dialogue? Oh, boy—I can. The voice inside my head can be so nasty! It knows my deepest fears and most nuanced triggers and it will *go for it* given the chance. The most intimate relationship you have is with yourself and, in turn, with that inner voice. To leave it unchecked, to let it run amok without getting to know it and setting some boundaries is devastating to your mental health. It needs your attention and you must create an intentional relationship with it as well.

When you do a search on Amazon for books about the inner critic, you see a lot of titles. Many of them are going to tell you how to slay it, banish it, conquer it, and annihilate it. There's even a book called *Retrain Your Brain: Seven Strategies to Fire Your Inner Critic* by yours truly. Yup. I fell for that advice early on, too. I spent so many hours battling my inner critic—all in the name of building a better business and improving my mindset for abundance.

Rubbish, I now say. Please don't kill your inner critic. It's a waste of time and energy. In fact, it is impossible. So learn how to approach it differently.

Let me share with you the journey of your inner critic in an exercise that I do with clients.

There's a part of your brain called the limbic brain or the limbic system, and it is the seat of emotion and memory. It is also in charge of survival responses and impulses such as fight, flight, feeding, fear, freezing up, and sex. The amygdala, which activates the fight-or-flight response, is part of the limbic system.

Humans learn through physical and emotional experiences. As children, we may get hurt when we touch a hot stove, or we may be hurt emotionally when someone close to us is mean, critical, or withholds love. We learn from both physical and emotional experiences.

When we burn ourselves on the stove our reaction is pretty straightforward. Our brain takes note. "That stove is dangerous—stay away from it!" By and large, most of us do, or at least we approach it with care thereafter. When someone we depend on for survival and safety is critical, mean, or harms us emotionally in some way (if we can't really take care of ourselves without this person) initially the amygdala will say, "That person is dangerous, stay away from him (or her)." But because you can't get away—for example, if you're a kid and you may live with this adult—then often what happens is that you internalize that adult's judgment of you. You're wrong, you shouldn't talk back, express your opinion or put your needs out there. Our reaction to a hot stove is our brain's need for survival, whereas our response to emotional hurt can become an internal echo of a voice that was drilled into our heads when we were children.

When I ask a client to tell me the origin story of her inner critic, she usually tells me the first instance of her experience of emotional shame. She'll also tell me that sometimes the voice in her head is still that person's voice. I also ask her how old she was when this happened and what she, as a little kiddo, needed in that instance. We then work together to go back internally and give it to her. We go through this process on many occasions at different ages until the client feels that she has mapped out the hot spots for her inner critic and what inner child experiences were connected with them.

It is not unusual to have a huge wall of sticky notes that looks something like this:

4 years: Father yelled at me and spanked me for wetting the bed.

> **Inner Kiddo:** Felt shame and needed to be reassured and tended to.

Inner Critic Voice: You are a mess, you cannot be trusted, you don't deserve a nice new bed.

7 years: Teacher scolded me in front of the class because I did not know how to read a word correctly while reading aloud. I was put into a remedial reading group.

Inner Kiddo: Felt shame, singled out and stupid.

Inner Critic Voice: Became the teacher's voice. "You are stupid and you need to be publicly shamed and separated from the group."

13 years: The girl in my friend group didn't invite me to her birthday party. She said that I was too loud and wanted too much attention.

Inner Kiddo: Felt excluded, humiliated and ashamed.

Inner Critic Voice: Became the 13-year-old friend's voice. "You are too loud, too much, who you are is not acceptable. You need to be quiet, listen and not seek attention."

By the end of this mapping exercise, people have quite the menagerie of voices connected to their inner critic, all with different scripts of why they are not good enough and need to be held back or managed in some way. What ends up happening, sadly, is that they begin to believe that those voices are who they are. We all take on the mantle of the inner critic, continuing the pattern from within.

By the end of that mapping, we also have a huge list of inner children that needed something that they did not get. Our inner critic does not really react differently to the threat of physical harm and the threat of emotional harm. Your inner critic is the protector of your inner kiddo. All it knows is that it somehow needs to keep you contained so that you don't get hurt by achieving success, whether it's starting a business, creating a product, giving a talk, or yes, writing a book. The fury with which my inner critic comes at me is as if I were considering scaling a mountain with no safety gear, jumping out a second story window, or eating a suspicious plant I see on a hike. It will try and stop me at all costs, including using my shame against me.

One thing I do to help my clients tame their inner critic is to give it a name. If we personify something, we can relate to it. We can talk back to it, and we can listen to it differently. What this exercise also does is it externalizes that inner critic. Then, and only then, can we stop believing that it's the core truth of who we are—because it's not.

Think about the voices in your head that battle you and hold you back, or torture you while you are doing the thing that feels risky. They can have many different energies, right?

Common Manifestations of the Inner Critic

Here are some of the most common voices that my coaching/therapy clients have shared with me.

The Worrier. The voice that is wringing its hands, worrying and saying I don't know if this is a good idea or not. Or "We have not heard back from that client— something must have gone wrong."

The Insecure Bluffer. The voice that is trying to talk you out of the thing you want to do by saying to you, "This is stupid. Why do you care about this anyway? It doesn't matter because it won't change anything."

The Annihilator. This is the voice that is most connected to your shame and it knows how to stop you in your tracks and show up in the most amazing ways to sabotage yourself. It is saying to you, "You are stupid, not popular, no one cares what you have to say, you won't survive this."

Each of these voices holds space in your head and shows up in different ways and each of them can be managed a little bit differently. But make no mistake: each of them has one job and that is to try and stop you. If the Worrier does not succeed and the Insecure Bluffer cannot stop you, the Annihilator will rise up and take its turn. Left unchecked, this is a vicious cycle. Luckily, there is another way.

As I mentioned earlier, your inner critic is the protector of your inner kiddo. That inner child is the part of you that experienced these shaming events and was taught that the experiences were not safe so therefore the child was not safe. Whenever your inner critic presents itself it is because one of your inner kiddos has been triggered and needs something.

The sad part is that we have not been taught this. We have been taught—by countless business motivation books—that the inner critic is a character flaw and needs to be destroyed. What we need to do instead is embrace it as a partner to our healing because there is a message there for us.

How different do you think your life and business would be if instead of beating yourself up for being triggered and then battling with your inner critic, you stopped and said. "I hear you. What message do you have for me? What do you need?"

It would be a game-changer.

The majority of the time, this is what happens when my clients and I stop the war, honor the voice and ask it what it wants.

When the inner critic steps aside, the message that's usually revealed is that some past self feels unsafe and needs some attention. In my practice, I help clients commune with that tender kid by doing an exercise that asks them to tap into moments from the past where they felt less than, shamed, or different in some way. Then we plot out which of those younger versions of themselves seem to be impacting their business, and we do a visualization. Let's say I had a 50-year-old client who wanted to go back to her 7-year-old self. We would create a space where my client could go back in time to connect with her 7-year-old self and spend time with her. She would close her eyes and see her, ask her what she needs to feel more safe, more loved, and more intelligent. And then she could talk to that younger self and say, "I hear what you're saying. I'm really sorry that happened to you. I'm your future self and I'm letting you know you're okay. That we're safe, that you're safe."

I'll never forget the day when I realized the power my inner kiddos had over my mood, my behavior, and ultimately, my business. I had been running my new business for about two years, and I was driving to a networking event—about an hour from my house—in the snow. I was aggravated and agitated from driving on slippery roads in low visibility. So when I got there, I was in a terrible mood. As a result, I didn't feel social, so I sat at a table in the very back of the room and did not engage with anyone. The inner critic in my head was talking a blue streak: about the stupid people at my table, about the person who was speaking from the stage. ("He doesn't know what he's talking about.") At one point, my inner critic even whispered in my ear, "I'm not going to participate in these ice-breakers, these are dumb!" The whole reason I had come to this event was to network. But I sat there, not participating, quietly judging everyone else in the room. Needless to say, I made no connections.

It felt like my body had been possessed by someone or something else. My adult self was there to make connections to improve my business and move it forward. On the drive home, I could not shake the feeling that I was not alone. Something was trying to get my attention. I was on the highway and I could not take it anymore, so I pulled over on the side of the road, turned off the car, and said, "What? What is it? Who is that?"

As clear as day I heard a voice in my head say, "Why do we have to keep doing this? It feels like the first day of school in the cafeteria every time, and we don't know where we belong."

I recognized in that moment that it was 10-year-old me who was in that networking meeting feeling lost and alone. And (bear with me here) another inner child, who's actually my 16-year-old self, took over (I've since named her Sadie). Sadie hates everybody and everything, so she is very connected to that inner critic. She's the one who put me in the bad mood, who said, "This is stupid! All these people are lame, this is a dumb event." Why did she interfere? Because she needed to protect the 10-year-old Nicole.

This was my *aha* moment—that the 10-year-old me was scared, and that she was replaying the circumstances in the cafeteria of feeling unloved and uncared for. And then my 16-year-old self—who was very much a rebel—was trying to protect *her*. When I realized this, I said out loud, "I am so sorry. I get that! I am so sorry that you, little 10-year-old Nicole, thought that you needed to be a part of this adult situation. Next time, I will make sure that I let you know that you can go play and you have no requirements or responsibilities in this adult scenario."

At future networking occasions, I dismissed Sadie, too (she is not good at networking). I say, "Listen, I've got this. You can go smoke behind the bleachers, I'll call you when I need you for something else."

Once you realize your inner kiddos are impacting the decisions you make in your business, you can talk to them and gently dismiss them with love.

The truth is that our inner critic is not a bully but a protector who deserves our attention and love. The sooner we learn how to do this, the sooner we are able to disrupt the inner critic pattern.

Life coach and author Martha Beck does something similar. In her book *Steering By Starlight*, she shares her technique of dealing with her anxiety and worry: she personifies both as a dragon. The dragon's name is Mo and it sits on her shoulder. Every time she starts to get in her head—feeling critical about who she is or something she wants to do—she recognizes it's not really her inner critic trying to hold her back. Rather than shaming herself, giving into the anxiety or complying with that critical voice, she will imagine that little dragon Mo. And she'll say, "Oh, Mo, I know you are anxious about this situation. I understand and it's going to be okay." Then she imagines feeding him some grapes and he sits quietly munching his grapes, because he has been acknowledged, seen and cared for. When Beck does that, she writes, the critical voice tends to go away.

When you can learn to love and honor your inner critic and all of the juicy, life-transforming information that it has for you, that's the gateway to emotional and financial success as well as sustainability for your business.

♥ ♥ ♥

Chapter 9

How to Love Your Money

I grew up in a Southern Baptist family in North Carolina. We were taught that money was not the most important thing to strive for and that both being of service and giving money away were virtues. One of the tenets of our church was that parishioners should be mission-oriented, which by default made me a giver. While I am no longer Southern Baptist, the impact of that upbringing is still with me today and for most of my life it has informed my decisions around money. Both of my sisters and I went into service-oriented careers, and I don't think that's a coincidence. I went on to get a B.S. in Community Service and Family Relations and a Master's Degree in Social Work. I always joke that I took a vow of poverty early on in my career and I'm okay with that. I never aspired to be rich or have lots of money.

But my relationship with money is not that simple. You see, not only was I raised in a Southern Baptist household, but

I also grew up religiously watching soap operas. Even my Pap watched *The Young and the Restless* and would record his shows if he had to be out so he could be sure to see what ol' Victor Newman was up to. I spent hours watching *The Young and The Restless* and *As the World Turns* with him. Both shows were about families staking out their wealth, and fighting over power and money. The wealthiest person in the room was usually the bad guy. To say that I grew up with complicated ideas about money would be an understatement.

To further this television education, I grew up in the '80s, watching shows like *Dallas*, *Knots Landing*, and *Dynasty* where people dripped with money and strove for excess at all cost. This money lust did have a very high cost in that it created chaos within the T.V. families, resentments and scandal. Where was the love?

When, where and how you grew up—including the kind of television you watched—all have an enormous impact on how you view money. Think about it right now. What were the phrases you commonly heard people say about money growing up? "Money doesn't grow on trees," "Money is the root of all evil," or—my personal favorite—"You can't have that unless you have a rich uncle who dies and leaves you money." Our views about money were shaped by those around us with unconscious phrases like these. From family, friends, and television characters, we picked up impressions about whether money is good or bad, safe or dangerous. All of those experiences have an impact on how we move forward as adults, especially regarding our relationship with money.

I started my coaching career with a focus on money and mindset, so I could write a whole book about this topic. Instead, I will give you some references at the end of this chapter for the best books on money and mindset.

One day, I was giving a talk at a monthly meeting for local women business owners on how childhood experiences and childhood trauma impact our relationship with money. During the Q&A part of the talk, a woman stood up, grabbed the mic and asked, "So you're telling me that my life now as an adult—including my money and how I earn and spend it—is all wrapped up in my childhood?"

I nodded, yes.

"I don't buy it," she said.

I asked her if I could ask her a few personal questions. "What is your favorite meal?"

"Lasagna," she said, not skipping a beat. "And not just any lasagna. It has to be my Nona's recipe. I still make it once a month for Sunday dinner."

"Do you follow a sports team?" I asked.

"Yes," she said. "The Pittsburgh Steelers all the way, we are a Steelers family. My Dad took us to some games back in the day and when we could not go we always watched on the T.V. together."

"Are you religious?" I asked.

"Yes, I'm a Catholic. I don't go to mass as much as I used to but I still see myself as a Catholic."

"So, where did you learn to love lasagna, the Steelers and the Catholic church?"

"My parents and grandparents—it's just how I was raised."

She stopped and was silent for a minute. Then, she said, "I get it. I am who I am and believe what I believe because of my childhood so why would money be any different?"

Exactly my point.

One of the biggest mistakes that a small business owner or entrepreneur can make is not examining their beliefs and behaviors around money that need to change. You must examine your relationship with money or you will have a difficult time making it, keeping it and feeling secure about it.

Here are the most common mistakes that I see small business owners and entrepreneurs making around money.

1. Not Examining Childhood Experiences. They have not examined the relationship between their childhood experiences around money and how they relate to it now. They have not asked themselves if they want this relationship to be different.

2. Having a Fixed Mindset. Their mindset about money is fixed and not open. Odd as it may sound, some people limit the amount of money that they can make, even going so far as to sabotage opportunities for making more money. One client, for example, was used to making $30,000 as a social worker. I watched her default to making that same amount, almost to the dollar, even when she switched professions. People who have this kind of mentally fixed limit don't ask for a raise, take on new projects, or seek new opportunities for expanding their income or their businesses.

3. Not Practicing Gratitude. They have not done the work to make gratitude a part of their daily practices and, as a result, they lose sight of how amazing each dollar they earn is. This has the potential to prevent them from earning more.

4. Choosing the Wrong Guides. They allow close-minded people to have input into the future of their business. You should share your financial goals with trusted advisors like a business coach or fellow entrepreneur. Steer clear of risk-averse family members (your mom, say, or that uncle who always puts his money in bonds). While it's understandable that you would want the buy-in of family members, some of them won't have a frame of reference for understanding the financial risks that you're taking so they may not be supportive of your goals.

5. Not Setting a Goal. They have not first set a financial goal and then set a big, toe-curling goal. Dreaming big and believing it is possible are skills to cultivate.

6. Not Examining Emotional Trauma. They have not examined any emotional trauma connected to difficulty or stress around money.

7. Willful Ignorance of Finances. Some business owners, afraid to learn that numbers are low, opt to ignore the financial details of their business altogether. Often, this fear is rooted in the belief that profitability equals worthiness and lack of profits equals unworthiness. Businesses wax and wane, so knowing the financials is crucial.

8. Not Having Boundaries. Some business owners give things away, underprice products or services, or change their price before even talking to potential clients. Others lack boundaries around their time—agreeing to meet other entrepreneurs for coffee before even finishing their own projects for the week. Remember: time is money. Don't squander either at the expense of your own success.

Never let someone tell you to charge what you are worth. Though it may seem a wise sentiment at first glance, it ultimately undervalues you. You are priceless. No amount of money can touch what you are worth. So make sure you set your money goals from a place that is congruent with the vision and mission that you and your business have agreed upon. For instance, if you want to be a solopreneur and your goals do not include making a lot of money, that's fine. Not everyone needs to have a seven-figure income.

♥

Money Trauma

Money trauma is any experience you had when you were a child that changed how you saw your security and safety in the world.

I have a client, Tammy, who had a degree in marketing but had chosen a career as a lifelong nanny. She worked for a wealthy family but never asked for a raise. We did some work and realized that she was stuck in a pattern of devaluing money because of trauma from her childhood.

When Tammy was seven, her father abandoned her, her sister and her mother. While he went on to get a really good job and own a beautiful house, Tammy and her sister and mom struggled to have any food leftover at the end of the week. When she went over to her father's house, he clearly didn't have to worry about money—he had, for example, two gallons of milk in the fridge. (Unlike Tammy who worried that one gallon wouldn't last through the end of the week.)

As a 7-year-old, Tammy said to herself, "Money will never be important to me. Because I will never be like him." She grew up valuing frugality. In fact, she became a dumpster diver and she shopped at thrift stores. She wore her poverty as a badge of honor.

What we determined in our work together was that every time she said yes to a nanny job, getting paid very little money, she was doing two things. She was rejecting money because she didn't want to be like her dad. But she was also saying to her 7-year-old self, "I pick you."

In effect, she was saying, "I choose you over money. You're more important."

When she became conscious of this pattern and recognized that she had deep trauma in her life around money, she was able to make a radical change. She left the low-paying nanny job and got a job in marketing, the field she had trained in. She also wrote a grant to get paid for the volunteer work she was already doing. By the end of that year, she had earned

$54,000 more because of that *aha* moment around early trauma with money.

♥

Best Money and Mindset Books

- *Tapping Into Wealth: How Emotional Freedom Techniques (EFT) Can Help You Clear the Path to Making More Money* by Margaret M. Lynch

- *You are a Badass At Making Money: Master the Mindset of Wealth* by Jen Sincero

- *The Soul of Money: Transforming your Relationship with Money and Life* by Lynne Twist

- *The Law of Divine Compensation: On Work, Money, and Miracles* by Marianne Williamson

- *The Big Leap: Conquer your Hidden Fear and Take Life to the Next Level* by Gay Hendricks

♥ ♥ ♥

Chapter 10

Creating an Emotional Sustainability Plan

When I worked as a clinical supervisor for a methadone clinic, I managed 12 counselors and I was responsible for a clinic with over 350 patients. Every day was full of crises, and I often had to make quick decisions due to the severity of our clients' conditions. Making matters more stressful, methadone is highly regulated in Pennsylvania, where I lived, and we could barely write a note or make a decision without having to check out what the state policy was so that we'd stay in compliance. A violation could cause a fine or, even worse, the loss of our license. These were high stakes, for sure.

Today, I work with clients who have invested in their own businesses and are challenged by all of the decisions and crises that show up for them, much as I was challenged at that methadone clinic. Each of my clients' futures and livelihoods depend upon the success of their business. I see clients drowning with no life vest, and struggling with no compass. The problem? They have not sat down to create a policy or procedure manual for themselves, much less an Emotional Sustainability Plan. Frankly, the idea never occurred to them. My client Beth, who was a money manager, was successful and very detail oriented. She was the kind of person who would leave nothing to chance; she knew every penny in her spreadsheets. Yet it never occurred to her to think about how she wanted to *feel* in her business. It never occurred to her to humanize herself within her business and make it a place where she would not only be successful but also enjoy it—and have a business that supported her. Once we created an Emotional Sustainability Plan for her, she felt supported and secure and her business became more than just a way to make money—it became a partner that helped her enjoy her life more.

What I know to be true about a successful, sustainable business is that it needs both a business plan and an Emotional Sustainability Plan. Creating an Emotional Sustainability Plan is crucial if you want to have a business that you love and that loves you back. This plan becomes a compass to help you make aligned daily decisions about your business. This plan is also helpful if you haven't yet created a policy manual or a procedure manual for your business because it informs how you make decisions in the future.

Create Your Emotional Sustainability Plan

Imagine that you are looking at a circle. Perhaps draw one so that you can see it clearly. Or, you can imagine the middle of a sunflower, or the hub of a bicycle wheel. Each petal or spoke coming out of that circle is a component of your Emotional Sustainability Plan.

Here are some examples of good spokes:

- Identifying and releasing the old relationship with your business.

- Defining and partnering with the new relationship that is loving and supportive.

- Clarifying your true values—not what you think they should be.

- Creating a vision and mission compass for you and your business that is aligned and feels true.

- Identifying your boundaries and where they have been flimsy. Learning to reinforce them with love and sovereignty.

- Knowing your inner critic and how it gets your attention. Partnering with it instead of letting it derail you.

- Learning to love your relationship with money and releasing the old stories and mindset about it. Creating a new money story that guides you.

It's important that you define, clarify, and lean into each one of these components of your business. If you do that, you will have a plan that you can return to each time you need to make a big decision, every time you are tempted to give in to someone else's demands, every time you look at changing your business model.

Your Emotional Sustainability Plan is designed to give you direction, courage, love, and support. It gives you guidelines for saying no when you need to, yes when you want to, and calling in love for yourself and your business every day.

I have a longstanding client who repeatedly said, "I wish that my employees would save up all their questions and put them in one email." My response was, "Don't make that a wish, make that a policy or procedure."

In fact, many of my clients think wistfully and longingly about what they want to have in their businesses. I say, "You get to have that!" But you have to set it up and ask for it, too. Your employees cannot read your mind; neither can your business. It's your job to set clear expectations. The deeper a client gets into learning about his Emotional Sustainability Plan, the less I have to say this because he has already defined this value or need and it is outlined in his plan. Someone with an Emotional Sustainability Plan won't just *wish* that his employees would send him bullet-pointed e-mails, he will ask employees to follow company procedure.

Plans are living, working documents. They grow and change as you and your business do, too. Your Emotional Sustainability Plan should mature as you do.

This book represents the work I do with my clients every day. It comes down to this: we have got to understand how childhood experiences impact the relationship we have with our business. Figuring this out requires clarity, awareness and intention. I hope that the questions, inquiries and exercises that I've shared in this book help you gain all three.

I know that it may have been a lot to take in on the first read. Return to the sections you were most resistant to, or where you felt the most discomfort. It's not realistic to integrate and master these concepts and tools overnight. So, I give you permission to put this book down feeling incomplete and needing to learn more. You can revisit the steps often. Whatever you do, please don't use any of the challenges you encountered here as tools to beat yourself up with. I don't want that for you and your business doesn't either.

If you had trauma in your childhood it will impact all of your relationships—and that includes the relationship that you are building with your business. But you can rise above the isolation and fear and find peace and prosperity in all aspects of your business, even the challenges. I'm confident that you will because you are not alone and you now have a plan. That is one of the reasons I encourage business owners to have a love fest with their business persona early in their journey. It takes time to develop a relationship with your business, but once you do it can grow.

My client Laura went through a radical transformation over the two years we worked together. When I first started seeing her, she was miserable. Though she had a very successful firm and wanted to take it to the next level, she hated managing her employees. She was impatient and reactive with them, and they ended up not liking her as a result. But she knew she couldn't build a successful business without employees.

As we went through the steps of my program together, she discovered that she had created her business to be like her father. Her father was a successful business owner who was also very rigid, demanding, explosive, and judgmental. He had very high standards that most people, including Laura, could not reach. In fact, no matter how successful Laura was, she felt it was not enough to impress her dad. She came to me because she wanted to work on her emotional reactions and reactivity to her employees. "I know I need employees to build out my business to reach this goal I have for myself," she told me.

I had her write a love letter to her business and one back from her business. She identified who those younger versions of herself were who were impacting her business. She identified her inner critic's voice and the multiple ways in which it showed up. She figured out how to listen to it but not be led by it, so she could pause and say, "I hear you. What do you need?"

When she realized that her revenue goal had merely been a way to get attention from her father, she let it go. Once she'd identified her values—connection, excellence and integrity— she recognized that instead of a revenue goal, she wanted a personal income goal instead. She also stopped beating herself up for not being able to manage her employees and hired an HR person. Eventually, she let go of her very complicated business model, laid off all her employees, and took on the parts of their jobs that she enjoyed. (She hired contractors to do the parts she did not like.)

During our entire time together, she always had a list of things she wished she didn't have to do. "I wish I didn't have employees. I wish I didn't have to write these reports all the time. I wish I didn't have to do payroll." And I said to her over and over, "You can have that, this is your business. Let's figure out how you can get there."

Today, Laura works 20 hours a week, if that. She doesn't have to manage employees. And she actually pulls in more income for herself than she did when she had employees. She gets to go on vacation with her husband now, whereas before she couldn't because she was working 60-hour weeks. And she has made space for herself because she identified what was depleting her and what energizes her, like taking classes or reading novels. If you saw her at the beginning of the time I worked with her—this driven, Type A, combative boss, trying to reach these external goals—to who she is now, she is unrecognizable. It was a complete turnaround.

That is my wish for you: Peace and prosperity and a business that you love and that loves you in return. As I say to my clients every day, "This is your business. You can have that!"

♥ ♥ ♥

Acknowledgments

It has been said that there are no new ideas, that each of us builds on the ideas and magic that came before us. I believe that this is true. We all stand on the shoulders of those who came before us. My hope is that my unique interpretation of all that I have learned—from reading and from lived experience—will inspire others to see their business in a new way.

Writing a book requires much time and effort on the author's part and in my experience just as much time, effort, and belief from those around me. I could not have written this book without a whole host of people who played distinct roles in making sure that I got this book out of my head. It has been rambling around in there trying to get out for over four years and I could not be more thrilled that it's finally seeing the light of day.

First and foremost, I would like to thank the clients, group members, and workshop participants who have contributed their stories to this book. These people have provided encouragement and feedback regarding this "love your business" concept, and have also urged me to continue speaking about the intersection of trauma and entrepreneurship.

Due to the confidential nature of my work, I will only use first names, but they know who they are and I am so grateful. Thank you, Susan, Brigitte, Janelle, Deb, Wanda, Angela, Michelle, Alethea, Megan, Marissa, Amanda, Christine, Abigail, Julie, Carrie, Stacey, Tina, Meighan, Kristin, Elaine, Melissa B, Mara, Debra, Alexis, Kae, Melissa O, and many others.

I also want to thank those who have played a role in birthing this book. I could not have done it without you. Joelle Hann and Hannah Wallace, thank you for the extra lengths you took to help me work around my learning difference to get the words out of my brain and onto the page. Your commitment to this project touched my heart. Thank you Danielle Baldwin for getting me started. Thank you to Charli Hoffman for your assistance in proofreading and enthusiasm about this book. Thank you Sarah Beaudin for your design work and expertise in navigating the publishing process.

As I mentioned, we stand on the shoulders of many, and I would like to thank my teachers and mentors who have been an important part in helping me step into my expertise. Lena West, thank you for trusting me with your people; Staci Jordan Shelton, thank you for showing me how to take up space; Tanya Geisler, thank you for your generosity and fierce love during hard times and good. Tara McMullin, thank you for that life-changing coffee date where you gave me the permission I was seeking to do something different, and thank you for giving me the spotlight and sharing your community with me.

Thank you Elizabeth Gilbert for writing *Big Magic* so I could have my magic moment. Thank you Brene' Brown. It has been an honor to train with you and to bring your Dare to Lead™ work into my community and into this book. Thank you Margaret Raniere for introducing me to trauma's impact on money so I could dig deeper and take it further.

I have been blessed to know some amazing people who have become friends, fans, and family. Thank you Patrice Dunckley for knowing my work better than anyone and for your support and friendship. Thank you Susan Dodge for being my soul sister and chosen family. Thank you, Marybeth Eyler and Candice Hozza for your friendship and love through some of the hardest months of my life. Thank you to the tiny consortium of Wanda Cox, Deb Coman, and Angela Todd. I love you all.

Thank you Carmen Hoffert for the daily existential conversations that keep me in the magic. Thank you Donna Cravotta for your friendship and vision. To my Dare to Lead™ Facilitator Family, you know who you are. Thank you to Megan Weisheipl and Jessica Barnak for your love and support and for holding me up—sometimes literally. (Like when my nerves get the better of me before public speaking.)

If I have not named you here and we have connected in some way around the Love Your Business process please know you are also a part of this book and its impact on the world.

I want to thank my family: Mom, Dad, Lesley, Kim, and Mary. Each of you contributed to this book in some way. The love I have for you is so very real. To my cousin, Michelle Lewis, thank you for every magical moment—from The Sparkle Hour podcast to the magic that happened in France—and for your fierce love and support.

Finally, I want to thank my husband Jason Keeber. He has been a witness to the most powerful moments of my life. He has inspired me to take my healing to the next level. He has provided me with safety so I could spread my wings. His love has comforted me in moments that I didn't think I could get through. When I got my breast cancer diagnosis I was terrified and still, I knew I would get through it because he was at my side. I made a vow to finish this book despite chemo, radiation—even a pandemic—and he has been there with me, every step. I mean it when I say that this book, this work, and this life would not be possible without him. Jason, you are my everything and I love you.

♥ ♥ ♥

Resources

- *Big Magic* by Elizabeth Gilbert

- *Dare to Lead* by Brene' Brown

- *Finding Your North Star* by Martha Beck

- *Steering by Starlight* by Martha Beck

- *The Deepest Well* by Dr. Nadine Burke Harris

- *Tapping Into Wealth* by Margaret Raniere

- *The Three Why*s by Nicole Lewis-Keeber

About the Author

Nicole Lewis-Keeber, MSW, LCSW is a thought leader, speaker, entrepreneur, and business coach. She is the founder of the Love Your Business School curriculum and the Do No Harm business intensive.

Nicole has combined her 18 years as a psychotherapist and five-plus years as a business therapist and coach to become the go-to expert on childhood trauma and entrepreneurship. She is a highly-sought-after speaker at entrepreneurship events and a variety of podcasts. She has been featured in Fast Company, TED-ED and on NPR and has a series of articles on Medium that outline how trauma can impact your business. Nicole has had conversations with over 250 business owners to research and define the impact of childhood trauma on business and has developed a framework for exploring the unique ways that trauma can show up in a business foundation.

Nicole grew up in the coastal town of Wilmington, North Carolina, and attended East Carolina University, where she earned her BS in Family and Community Service. Later, she attended Widener University, where she received her Master's in Social Work.

Nicole is a survivor of childhood trauma and breast cancer and she is striving to live as a neurodivergent person in a neurotypical world.

She lives with her husband and two boy kitties, Critter and Yum Yum, in Lancaster, Pennsylvania.

♥ ♥ ♥